MY TALUS

By Dr. Mitzi Williams
with Dr. Matthew Dobbs and Dr. Scott Kaiser
Illustrated by Ginger Nielson

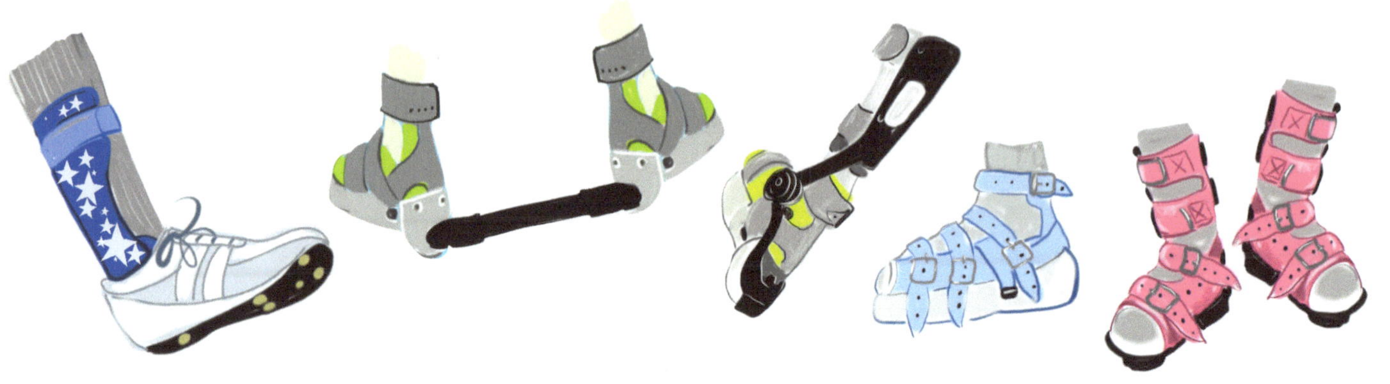

MY TALUS

ISBN-13: 979-8-9850842-2-1
Mitzi Williams Publisher

Mitzi Williams DPM, FACFAS is a pediatric foot and lower extremity surgeon who specializes in congenital deformities. Dr. Williams and her colleague, Dr. Scott Kaiser, direct the Pediatric and Infant Foot Deformity Clinic at Kaiser Permanente in Oakland, California. She is an attending surgeon at the SF Bay Area Foot and Ankle Residency Program. Dr. Williams is nationally recognized for her expertise in treating pediatric foot and lower extremity deformities.

Matthew Dobbs MD, FACS is the director of the Dobbs Clubfoot Center at the Paley Institute in West Palm Beach, Florida. Prior to that, he was the Dr. Asa C. and Mrs. Dorothy W. Jones Professor of Orthopaedic Surgery and the Director of Strategic Planning at Washington University School of Medicine. Dr. Dobbs is internationally recognized for his expertise and innovation in the field of pediatric foot and lower extremity deformities.

Scott Kaiser MD is a pediatric orthopedic surgeon who specializes in a wide breadth of disorders that affect children's gait. He partners with Dr. Mitzi Williams to direct the Pediatric and Infant Foot Deformity Clinic at Kaiser Permanente in Oakland, California.

We thank our incredible clinical and surgical care teams including Kathy Kreitner, Marissa Bard, Anna Pacheco, and Omar Phillips.

We give special thanks to the patients and their families whose stories inspire us.

MY TALUS, is dedicated to the children worldwide born with vertical talus. This book shares a child's perspective on the condition and provides accurate information for their families. We find this book will be a helpful tool in speaking with children about vertical talus. This book is also helpful in aiding in any conversation with siblings and friends of children with vertical talus.

Hi! My name is Ryden.

I am happy, playful, and kind!

Like some of you, I was born with vertical talus.

Vertical talus means that my feet turn outward and need help to become more straight.

Feet come in all shapes! Some feet go in while my feet go up and out. Some feet are flat but my feet have no arch at all!

My doctor said my talus and foot are not
in the best position.

As a baby, my doctor applied well-molded casts to my feet that came all the way up on my thighs.

My knees were bent to stop my casts from slipping off.

While some children do not have vertical talus, others are born with vertical talus affecting one or both feet. My friend has vertical talus on his right foot and clubfoot on his left foot!
Can you find the ladybug?

My casts were changed weekly for five
weeks. Some children need more casts.

Once my feet looked more straight,
I underwent a procedure to help my feet
even more. My final casts were applied
afterwards.

There are pictures of my family with
me at every doctor's visit.

While I do not remember my casts or procedure, I am proud of my boots. I wear wonderful boots to help keep my feet straight while I grow.

I call them my magical bedtime boots and I will sleep in them. Without them, my feet may turn out again.

I always sleep in my boots! Come dream with me!

Tonight I will dream of an incredible camping trip under the night sky. The stars will shimmer above while we roast gigantic marshmallows.

Next we will take a boat ride among the rainbow-colored fish.

The dolphins will splash in the waves and play all around me! The palm trees sway in the breeze.

Finally, I will dream of a magical land of toys.
Every toy imaginable will be there. Let's play!

POLICE
POLICE

I have incredible boots and my future
looks bright with my boots on.

Fun Facts

• Vertical talus (CVT) is defined as a more rigid rockerbottom flat foot. The foot is in valgus along with equinus (tight achilles tendon).

• The Dobbs Method, founded by Matthew Dobbs MD, contains a series of maneuvers to manipulate the foot into an improved position. Well-molded casts are generally changed weekly. The method is utilized to treat vertical talus and recurrences.

• Upon correction, children undergo a surgical procedure under general anesthesia in an operating room. The talonavicular joint is pinned and the achilles tendon is released. A cast is applied. A child is then casted for about 6 weeks with skin checks scheduled.

• Bracing is then initiated and continued until two years of age. Stretching the foot down and inwards is helpful daily.

• Vertical talus can be recurrent. Bracing helps minimize recurrence while some children will still develop return of vertical talus features. It is important to maintain close follow up with the child's physician.

- Some children may need surgical procedures to rebalance the foot.

- Children with rigid deformities may require other procedures to realign the foot.

- Some children with neurologic and or motor weakness may require specific daytime bracing to promote stability and function along with nighttime bracing to minimize contractures and recurrence.

- ADMs may be used in the setting of neuromuscular conditions with hip and or knee contractures. Research is ongoing for use in younger patients.

For more information please visit:
drmitziwilliams.com, **dobbsclubfoot.com**
dobbsbrace.com, and **kiddfoot.com**

The talus, like a whale, likes to come
up and spout.
My talus is like a whale stuck in a net,
and needs help to get out.

The doctor said she'll release the net
to set my talus free.
And my free talus will move up and down
as I jump happily.

Have some fun with
these coloring pages.

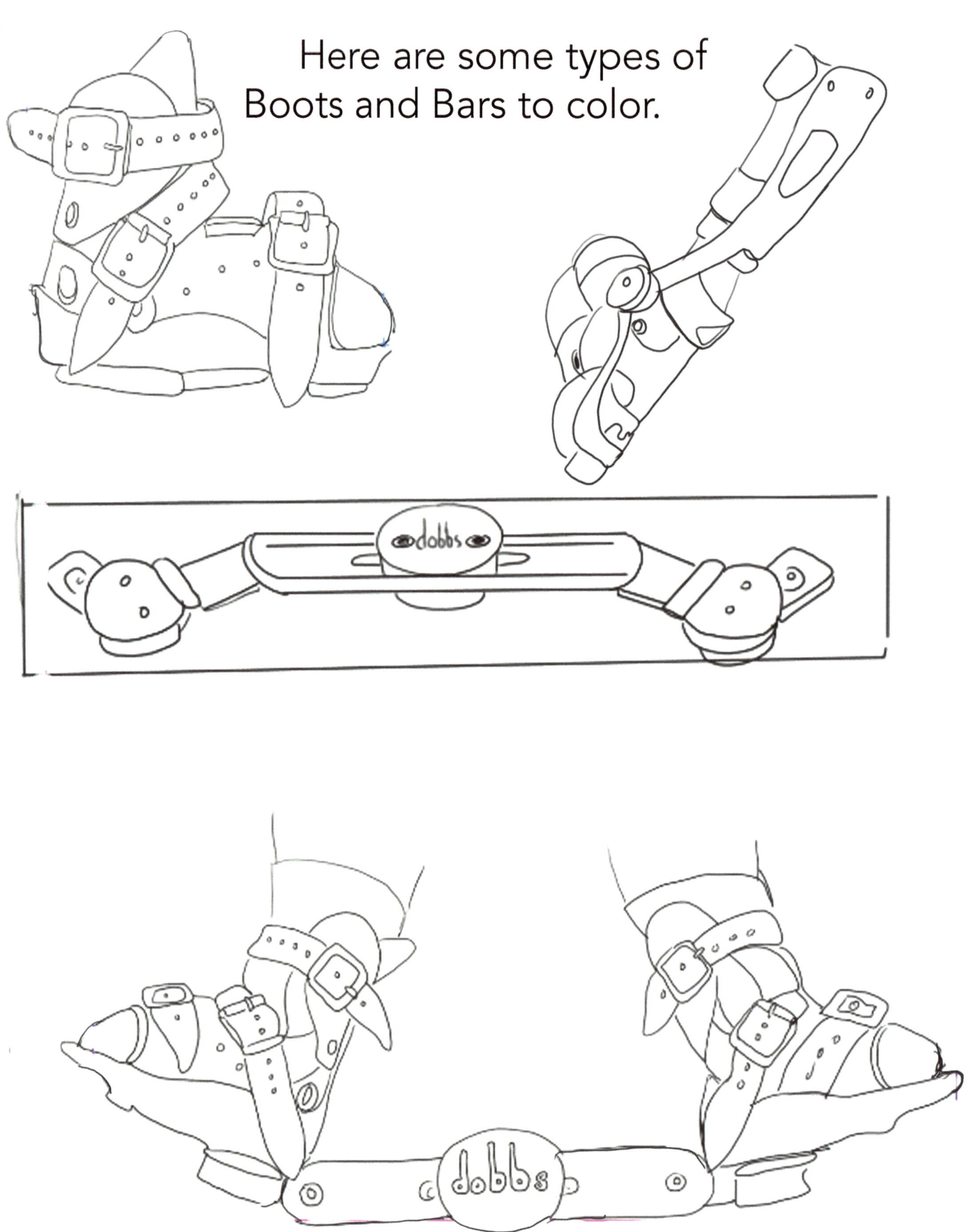

Here are some types of
Boots and Bars to color.
dobbs
dobbs

We want you to meet
Dr. Dobbs's pup, Ignacio.
Can you find him in this book?
Look for him on pages 4,13 and 27.